WHOSE LIFE IS IT

ANYWAY?

WHOSE LIFE IS IT ANYWAY?

A Selection of Poems

Written By

THEODOSIA SOTERIOU

authorHOUSE®

AuthorHouse™ UK Ltd.
1663 Liberty Drive
Bloomington, IN 47403 USA
www.authorhouse.co.uk
Phone: 0800.197.4150

Published by AuthorHouse   09/23/2014

ISBN: 978-1-4772-3903-2 (sc)
ISBN: 978-1-4772-3904-9 (e)

This book is printed on acid-free paper.

Dedicated to
Family & Friends

CONTENTS

HOW RICH WE ARE!

When you proposed, I wasn't sure
Just what I ought to do,
I wanted someone handsome
And not at all like you.

I wanted someone tall and rich
And strong and dominating,
But you were short and timid
And not one for debating.

It seemed to me that I was young
With lots of time to choose,
I didn't think that, as your wife,
I'd fit into those shoes.

But here we are, we're married
And happy as could be,
It goes to show you just can't judge
By what shows outwardly.

I see now you have kindness
And patience true galore,
I see a heart so full of love
How could I want for more?

I wonder now the value
Of good looks, wealth and charm,
We have each other, you and I,
We're rich in that alone.

Asleep Like a Baby

I sit in an office for most of the day
Get on with my duties the usual way
The phone rings, I answer, "This is 2095"
"Sorry, wrong number" the caller replies.

When I am not busy, with little to do
I'm longing for home-time to be back with you
I sigh and I wander and look at the clock
Then wish I hadn't—it gives me a shock.

I think of you lonely from three until five
And with all my heart I wish I could skive,
But sadly I cannot and here I must stay
Until I have come to the end of the day.

I rush home to find you and what do I see
Asleep like a baby upon the settee
A cigarette burning, a drink on the floor
And you don't even hear when I open the door.

You wake with a start and you kiss me hello
And with that my body with warmth it does glow
You sip at your coffee, I make it just right
And then you are off to your job in the night.

I sit there and think what to do with myself
The housework, the cooking, there isn't much else
And then when I'm done and I sit by the Telly
I wonder what happened to my old friends and Nelly.

The time it does drag, at home and at work,
And I'm always nervous alone when it's dark
But I know that you will come home in a hurry
When you have finished and earned your day's money.

And when you come home to me what do you see
Asleep like a baby upon the settee
The record still playing, a book on the floor
And I don't even hear when you open the door.

3

MARRIED TO A STRANGER

I'm married to a stranger
And don't know how or why,
I thought we knew each other well
But was it all a lie?

He never wants to talk to me
I don't laugh at his jokes,
We have nothing in common
Has it all been a hoax?

We have three grown up children
And grandchildren to boot,
But I can't say he's romantic
And I never thought him 'cute'.

We're old and grey and weary
And, despite all the goodwill,
All we do is argue;
But we're together still.

I guess when we were married
It was "till death us do part"
"For better or for worse"
Is engraved upon my heart.

You always hurt the one you love
So, if this saying's true,
I guess he really must love me
And I must love him too.

EACH OTHER'S VALENTINE

I know you think I am a pain
And, probably, you're right,
I know I'm awkward to a fault
And that is why we fight.

I may expect too much from you
And call you daft and lazy,
But it is the little things
That always drive me crazy.

I want to feel that we are close
That you are my best friend,
I need to feel I'm special
That you'll love me to the end.

We've been together long enough
We've passed the test of time,
And that's why we will always be
Each other's Valentine.

LOVE IS BLIND

All my life I have believed
True love would come my way,
I lived in hope and fantasised
I waited for the day.

How earnestly, yet patiently
Have I survived these years,
Not knowing when my time would come
And holding back the tears.

And yet, my love was always there
So steadfast, strong and true,
How did I not recognise
That my true love was you?

Day in, day out, year after year
You walked one step behind,
I cannot help but wonder
How I could have been so blind.

I hope you will forgive me
And that we can start anew,
Let's make up for the years gone by
And prove our love is true.

LET ME

Let me thank the hands that held me
When my body pain did feel;

Let me touch the face that smiled
When tears were all that mine would yield;

Let me see the eyes that looked
So confident that I would live;

Let me kiss the lips that whispered
Loving words that strength did give;

Let me lean against the man
Who stood by me through thick and thin;

Let me open wide my arms
And let the man I love come in.

LOVE'S ALPHABET

'A' for Admiring, when beauty we see
'B' for Believing that you love me
'C' for Caring when times are hard
'D' for Daring to make you mad
'E' for Everything that we treasure
'F' for Finding time for leisure
'G' for Growing close to each other
'H' for Helping our fellow brother
'I' for Including me in your life
'J' for Joyous that I'm your wife
'K' for Keeping nothing from me
'L' for Loving eternally
'M' for Meaning the words that you say
'N' for Needing me every day
'O' for Opening the door to your heart
'P' for Promising that we'll never part
'Q' for Quietly taking life as it comes
'R' for Readily making romance
'S' for Sharing all we've got
'T' for Trusting—Yes, why not?
'U', of course, for Understanding
'V' the Voice that's so demanding
'W' for Wonderful
'X' I think I'll leave to you!
'Y' for Yearning ever so, and
'Z' for Zeal, wherever you go.

WEDDING BELLS

The Wedding Bells will toll for you
Come sun, high wind or shower,
So listen to these words of mine
In this, your greatest hour.

I wish you luck and happiness
And a most joyous day,
But don't forget the difference
Between work and rest and play.

And when you are a wife at last
You must do what you ought,
But if you don't, then do take care
That you are never caught!

And if you are, remember me
Because, as well you know,
I will be the first to say
That I told you so!

So please be very careful
And look after your new toy,
Sincerely though, joking aside,
I wish you lots of joy.

FOREVER BY YOUR SIDE

This happy day has come at last
To join the future with the past
We know your love is deep and true
And this is what we wish for you.

We wish you happiness and health
We wish you joy, success and wealth
We wish you all that you desire
Each day to reach a little higher.

Love is all about respect
Love means never to neglect
Love is loyal, your best friend
Love is faithful to the end.

So let us raise our glasses
To you and your new bride
May your love grow from strength to strength
Forever by your side.

MOTHERHOOD

The joys of motherhood will soon
Be knocking at your door,
A healthy bouncing baby
- Who could want for more?

Two eyes that seem to follow you
(Although they still can't see),
And, guess who's always holding her
- When she wants a wee?!

You place a finger in her hand
She grips and won't let go,
You feel so proud and needed
- It's quite something, you know.

She may not let you sleep at night
And demand attention all day,
It's something you'll get used to
- You'll soon learn how to play!

But when you watch her sleeping
And you feel sure she's just grinned,
Don't get too excited
- You see, it's only wind!

IT'S A BOY!

Oh me! Oh my!
What can I say,
Your dream came true
That happy day,
As tears of pain
Were shed for joy,
When you gave birth
To your baby boy!

How small, how sweet,
How perfect, too,
The magic link
To both of you,
To watch him smile,
To watch him sleep,
These are all moments
You will keep.

And as you watch him
Learn and grow,
And wonder what
He'll be, you'll know
That, whatever he does,
Wherever he may go,
You will always
Love him so.

LUCKY ME

In all the world there cannot be
A luckier girl than me
In all the world there are but few
That share my kind of glee
For what's in store for me is not,
I think you will agree,
The kind of thing that's thought of
As most people's "cup of tea"!

Once more a mother I'm to be
But it's twice the joy I'll bear
Whatever hardships come my way
I will not despair
For, although it's 'double trouble'
(And I've had more than my share)
My twins, they will not suffer
They'll have twice the love and care.

I'm only strong because I know
That wealth is not the key
To health and true contentment
- I'm lucky to be me!
So all else does not matter
For it's happy I shall be
And everything will be worthwhile
When I'm a mum of three.

MOTHER

Mother
The sweetest word that one can say
That stirs the heart in every way
When uttered by a child so dear,
A word that's music to the ear.

Mother
The one that cannot help but love
Her offspring gifts from up above,
The one who'd be prepared to die
To keep them safe on land and sky.

Mother
The smile of whom comes from the heart
Which often breaks when kids depart,
The smile which brightens up the day
When given in that special way.

Mother
Whose love will always keep us warm
Protecting us from every storm,
Without whom we would feel the cold;
A mother is worth her weight in gold.

Mother
Unique and irreplaceable
Unselfish and dependable,
Whose faith in us will never fade;
All this can never be repaid.

ANASTASIA
(Birth of a Granddaughter)

My heart expands with sheer delight
Each time I see your face,
You've brought a joy into my world
Which nothing can replace.

You are a wonder to behold
A product of true love,
You are the hope of times to come
A gift from God above.

You are the breath I take to live
You are my sound and sight,
You are the music that I make
You turn the dark to light.

May you grow to be a beauty
May you have good sense and grace,
May your heart be full of goodness
And be just, in every case.

May you have the strength and courage
Your true feelings to pursue,
May you grow with love and wisdom
And succeed in all you do.

SEEMS LIKE ONLY YESTERDAY

It seems like just the other year
That I was newly wed,
It seems like just some months ago
My kids were born and bred,
It seems like only a few weeks
Since I became a gran,
How did I achieve all this
In such a short time span?

It seems like just the other day
I started my first job,
And now, all these years later
I almost want to sob,
I want to know what happened
To all those years between,
It seems like only yesterday
That I was Sweet 16.

But now my hair is turning grey
And I have put on weight,
The wrinkles are starting to show
And I'm past my 'sell-by-date',
My husband, kids and grandchildren
Have brought me joy—and pain,
But, thanks to them, I can be sure
My life is not in vain.

OH, TO BE SLIM!

Oh, to be slim and tummy-less
Oh, to be free from fat
Oh, to look good in bikinis
And shorts and things like that.

Oh, for a beautiful figure
Oh, for a waist so petite
Oh, for the legs of a model
And pretty, tiny feet.

What would we have to sacrifice
For a figure so divine?
Cakes and biscuits would have to go
And so would cheese and wine.

We'd have to curb our eating
We'd have to do without sweets
We'd have to live on vegetables
And starve ourselves for weeks.

We'd not be allowed potatoes
We'd not be allowed to eat bread
We couldn't have sugar in our tea;
We may as well be dead!

This is what must be sacrificed
For a figure as nice as that,
So, girls, what would you rather be?
—Miserable, or FAT?

COLLEGE

When I was at college
Improving my knowledge
Of things I knew little about,
I listened to teacher
As though he were preacher
While others would laugh and would shout.

They'd think I was loony
To listen to Mooney
And get extra work to take home,
But I knew that soon
It would be end of June
And results of exams would be known.

And when the time came
They'd be going insane
With anxiety and nervousness,
"What if we should fail?"
They'd exclaim, going pale,
But they'd shrug it off nevertheless.

We'd meet the next year
So full of good cheer
Until we exchanged our results,
They'd laugh at each other
For wasting another
Whole year in just boozing and jokes.

They'd look at me slyly
And wonder if really
I'd managed to get my Diploma,
The doubt, it was there,
Filling the air
So thick it was like an aroma.

But boast I did not
Or else they would plot
Against me, and that would not do,
So I merrily went
To the class to torment
- I was teacher and nobody knew!

HOMEWORK

The term has begun
And I haven't done
The homework I was set to do,
I've not had the time
To read but a line
Of homework—honest, it's true!

I get home from work
It is almost dark
There's dinner to cook and to serve,
The washing needs doing
A button needs sewing
And I've got to read?—What a nerve!

I have good intentions
These aren't just inventions
I really do wish I could do it,
But try as I might
The day turns to night
And I find I just can't spare a minute.

Whenever I sit down
To rest for a short while
I remember my homework is waiting,
But the effort is great
So I just let it wait
- The bones in my body are aching!

"I'll do it tomorrow"
I say with some sorrow
For I know that this won't be true,
"I won't be so busy"
Says I feeling dizzy
"I've only the ironing to do!"

So Thursday arrives
And I'm making dives
As everyone hands in their work,
I get a sly look
And I hide in my book
While the others try not to smirk.

This week I'll be good
I'll make time, like I should,
I will not give it a miss,
Oh, why pretend?
I know it's the end
- It's my state of marital bliss!

19

THAT'LL BE THE DAY!

Whenever the weather
Is breezy and bright
And the day takes much longer
To turn into night,
Whenever the birds
Seem to sing without rest
That'll be the day
I'll be at my best.

When walking reminds me
I'm breathing fresh air
And the sunshine helps me
Forget I've a care,
When eating a salad
Is more than enough
That'll be the day
I'll most want to laugh.

When out-of-door sport
Sounds like good fun
And I'm told what a good job
My diet has done,
When wearing bikinis
No longer offend
That'll be the day
I'll not want to end.

That'll be the day!

I Am What I Am

I speak my mind, I tell the truth
I do not make pretences,
I criticise and tantalise
And make people defensive.

Feelings of disapproval show
On my face and in my manner,
And anger can be never hid
- I hold it like a banner!

I want to be seen as I am
And not as I should be,
I'd like to be accepted
Not as 'his wife', but as ME.

My words may be a little sharp
My manners may be lacking,
But in my heart there's honesty
Of that, there's no mistaking.

So please don't be offended
If I'm speaking out of turn,
It's not something I'm proud of
And I'm still trying to learn.

The only consolation is,
If I can be so bold,
At least, with me, you can believe
Whatever you are told!

FRIENDS

It's nice to have friends to talk to
It's nice to have friends so kind,
It's nice to have friends who listen
To what you may have on your mind.

It's nice to have friends so eager
To help and give you advice,
It's nice to be able to share
Your problems, your trouble and strife.

It's nice to have shoulders to cry on
Whenever you are in the need,
It's nice to have one to rely on
To do you a good deed.

It's nice to have friends so caring
And anxious to see you through,
It's nice to have friends so thoughtful
It's nice to have friends like you.

DEAR DENTIST . . .

When I first came to visit you
I trembled much with fear
Because I knew that I would not
Like what I had to hear.

You said I needed fillings
So many, I lost count,
You also said a golden crown
Was really paramount.

This came to me as quite a shock
It's not what I expected,
You made me feel deeply ashamed
That my teeth I had neglected.

I understand your attitude
Towards people like me,
I know you cannot sympathise
But, please listen to my plea.

I only came to you because
My friend said you were good,
And I accept her word for that
- As many people would.

So please can you get on with it,
What must be, must be,
Just do me a little favour and
- Be gentle with me!

HYPOCHONDRIA?

I've got an empty feeling in my tum
My heart is very heavy
My legs are weak
And certainly
Do not hold me steady.

I'm cold and shivery all day long
My hands shake when I'm writing
My throat is sore
My nose is raw
This cold I'm fed up fighting.

I've got these spots all up my arms
My legs have caught them too
They itch like mad
They're really bad
I don't think I'll pull through!

My friends say it's an allergy
My doctor thinks it's flees
Some even say
They'll go away
If I rub my knees!?!

Heat rash has been suggested
And German Measles too
But I think today
Is the time to say . . .
"It's been nice knowing you!"

IN TIMES TO COME

How I love to run around
On England's finest grass
And listen to the singing birds
Whenever trees I pass.

How I love the smell of leaves
When they are damp with dew,
And the buzzing bumble bees
When they have work to do.

How I love the sky at night
It's full moon high above,
When each star winks at you in turn
With promises of love.

How I love the riverside
When all is still and calm,
To watch the water pass me by
And lose all track of time.

All these things I love to see
To touch and to enjoy,
I wonder if, in times to come,
These things we'll not destroy.

THE COUNTRYSIDE

I strolled along the countryside
Alone and feeling sad
But when I saw the beauty there
All I could feel was glad.

The flowers swayed in perfect time
Their heads held high with pride,
Indeed, the sight was so sublime
I very nearly cried.

I wandered further down the lane
And there, before my eyes,
To my delight, an awesome sight
Of dancing butterflies.

A rainbow bright with colours bold
Of blues and reds and yellows,
A sight of wonder to behold
For any worthy fellows.

A carpet laid of mystic greens
As far as I could see,
Until it met the sky so blue
Deep as eternity.

And when I stopped to listen there
And heard the birds in throng,
The nightingales and larks alike
Did fill my heart with song.

I strolled along the countryside
To realise, at last,
That loneliness does not belong
To the future, but the past.

SUN, WIND, RAIN AND SNOW

A beautiful sight to behold
The sun, with its rays of gold,
It ages not, it's oh, so hot,
It's lovely and bright and bold.

The wind with its howling at night
Is enough to give you a fright,
But during the day, when it is at play,
It's cool, not too rough, but just right.

The pitter-patter of rain,
Is a sound we hear over again,
As its glistening drops land on our rooftops
The puddles below remain.

But what do we think of our snow?
It doesn't come often, I know,
But the breathtaking sight of that brilliant white
Makes me wish it would never go.

CRY FOR PEACE

Why can't we ever be content
With what we have at hand?
Why are we always looking for
That extra bit of land?

What difference would it make to have
Acres of land galore?
If less suffices all our needs
Why do we still want more?

Why can't we live in peace and love
Each home its own safe haven?
To live and let live, day by day,
And keep away the mayhem.

Is it too much to hope for peace?
Must we be full of hate?
Why can't we show respect for life
Before it is too late?

Warning To Mankind

Why is it that we've been warned
Against future destruction,
If not to give us all a chance
To take corrective action.

We can have no excuses
And there can be no surprise
When foreseen prophecies come true
Before our very eyes.

We have the opportunity
To put right what is wrong,
All we need is courage,
To be wise and to be strong.

Let us learn to love each other
Banish wicked thoughts and deeds,
Let us live like friends, together,
Follow where the right path leads.

Let us treasure every minute
That we have on this dear earth,
Let's not waste a single moment
To appreciate its worth.

The power is in our very hands
A gift from God above,
The strongest force in all the world
The power and strength of Love.

We owe it to our children
To stranger and to brother,
We owe it to humanity
We owe it to each other.

29

WHERE THERE'S LOVE, THERE'S BLISS

When all around are thinking of
What fortunes lie in store,
Your mind is only on one thing
- To be prepared for war.

When everyone is dreaming of
What fate the future brings,
Your thoughts are just preoccupied
With fundamental things.

You want to be prepared to fight
To stand up for your land,
To hold your head up high and know
That you, too, had a hand.

A hand defending common rights
Reclaiming what was yours,
A hand that you believe will help
To open many doors.

But this is not the way to win
It's not how to survive,
This road can only lead to death
And then—Who'll be alive . . . ?

Who will there be to see the land
That young men fought and died for?
Who will be left to repossess
The homes that we all cried for?

But even if we could reclaim
The homes that we had built,
It surely could NEVER be worth
The blood that would be spilt.

Home is where the heart is
So please remember this,
It's only love that conquers all
And where there's Love, there's Bliss.

HOW SORRY WE SHALL BE!

The way I see things, all around,
We never should have been
Allowed even to walk the ground
Or sunshine to have seen.

For what thanks do we offer
To God in Heaven above
Who gave us flowers and trees and things
And taught us how to love?

We just take for granted
All the things we see,
But when our time has come to go
- How sorry we shall be!

A Toast To Sheila Gray

It's 1957
And the future's looking bright
She joined a company of Greeks
And didn't flee in fright.

Despite our eccentricities
She took things in her stride
She proved her worth and steadfastness
- This cannot be denied.

She's been through all the good times
And helped us through the bad
She stood by us through thick and thin
Through happy and through sad.

A 'Mother Hen' she's been to us
And 'clipped our ears'—not 'alf
She'd not take any nonsense
From Directors or from Staff.

The firm will never be the same
Without her helping hand
Her loyalty and our gratitude
On a pedestal will stand.

So now, as we reflect upon
Her years with R & K
Please stand and raise your glasses
For a toast to Sheila Gray!

STAR DINNER

Pleased to meet you, one and all
I trust you've had a ball,
We've tried to cater for all tastes
Big appetites and small.

I'm really pleased to be here
And see my efforts through,
I've tried to think of everything
I should and shouldn't do.

I learned a lot from colleagues
When they showed me last year's moves,
This year, EK has been my guide
And I hope that he approves.

I cannot take full credit though
For EK has done his bit,
He told me where to book
What to eat and where to sit.

But responsibility is mine
For all that has been hired,
'Cause, should the evening not succeed
'Tis I who will be fired!

Job Satisfaction

I like the banter and the cheek
I like to have a laugh
I like to crack a joke or two
With the bosses and the staff.

But when it comes to actual work
It is no laughing matter
I know just where my duty lies
And that is with the latter.

However, due to issues
That require corrective action
I cannot see this working
As I've no job satisfaction.

It's therefore with utmost regret
This job I must decline
I feel my skills are wasted here
And I'm running out of time.

I really need to move on now
To try and find my niche
I wish you all every success
And hope you will 'capisce'!

OVER THE HILL?

I may be getting older
But I'm not 'over the hill'
I'm young at heart and tend to thrive
On challenge and goodwill.

I'm young enough to work hard
And old enough to know
That loyalty and commitment
Will always run the show.

I don't mind if I work late
(The kids are grown you see)
And working under pressure
Is just my cup of tea!

I've always enjoyed working
With or without the frills
And, so far, I have never
Had cause to doubt my skills.

So . . .

Don't write me off too quickly
Please see my point of view,
All I ask is for a chance
To show what I can do!

ANOTHER YEAR

Another year has just gone by
And still I'm where I started,
To pastures new, I'm pleased to go
Until I must be parted.

I give my all, and all are sad
When I must 'shake a leg',
But so far all the posts are round
- And I am a square peg!

I'm pleased to carry on as is
Until I find my niche,
Why should I accept a pie
When I'd prefer a quiche?

I know I'm choosy, to a fault,
I may be splitting hairs,
But if I've missed a job or two,
The greater loss is theirs!

However, there is nothing more
I'd like to have than this;
To find my ideal job (and boss)
And realise my wish.

TO THE BOSS

They said it wasn't easy
To find somebody who
Would meet your expectations
And be a 'hit' with you.

They said you needed someone
Who was pretty thick-skinned
Someone who knew when to duck
And clear your 'second wind'.

Well, I'm the one you picked on
For this most dubious honour
So I shall have to rise to it
Or else I'll be a 'goner'.

I hope that I can prove to you
That you have chosen well
For I can't resist a challenge
I'm a fighter—can't you tell?

I may have tripped up, once or twice
But what you say is true
Mistakes are there to learn from
And that's what I will do.

At the risk of going on a bit
I would just like to mention
If I've ever spoken out of turn
It's with the best intention.

So please don't be offended
Now that all is said and done
For I hope we'll work together well
For many years to come.

JOURNEY TO WORK

I answer the telephone, don't let it ring
I type and I file and I do everything,
But what do I get at the end of the day?
"Home-time already, are you off again?"

I know I'm not punctual, but I don't get behind,
My work is important and I do not mind
If I have to work late or miss my lift home,
I feel it's my duty, the choice is my own.

I do leave home early, I don't get up late,
It's just that my bus likes to lengthen my wait
And when I arrive at the station, I know
That my train will, as usual, be long overdue.

And whilst on my journey and I still have a chance
The train will not hurry, it moves in a trance,
It stops and it starts till at last I arrive
At Dagenham Heathway—barely alive!

I run to the exits and hand in my ticket
Charge through the traffic and—yes—I just miss it!
My bus it is there at the stop, I can see,
But I am afraid it runs faster than me!

I wait for the next one, I have but no choice
My chances of starting on time are a loss,
I stand in the cold till I can't feel my thumbs
And then, after ages, the 'Ford Works' bus comes.

I now have to walk from Gate Number One
Whilst cars overtake I'm picked up by no-one,
My feet, they are frozen, I feel I could shout
I've done yet no work, but I'm already worn out!

I try to be early, but always I fail
I sometimes imagine they'll send me to jail
But what should I do, if I can't start on time?
Hand in my Notice?—Resign?

WARNING TO ALL NEWCOMERS

We are in surroundings
So gloomy and cold,
The lane to the office
Is hard to behold,
When lorries or vans
One do pass in their haste,
A cloud of black dust
Will be blown in one's face.

The journey to work
Will be hard to endure,
But on one's arrival
There'll be given a tour,
And once well acquainted
With 'What', 'Where' and 'When',
It's no longer permitted
To ask questions again.

The muck in the river
And the derelict sites,
The lane in deep darkness
As there are no lights,
This is but a sample
Of what is in store,
- But first, sign the contract,
Then we'll tell you some more!

DANCE

When I am on the dance floor
I'm in another world,
My spirit lifts, my mind is free
And stresses are unfurled.

I love to dance the Quickstep
The Samba and the Waltz,
The Jive, the Paso Doble
And the Cha Cha Cha, of course.

The Foxtrot and the Rhumba
Are the hardest ones to master,
For no matter how you're feeling
They just won't go any faster.

If you really want the rhythm
It's the Salsa or the Mambo,
But you cannot beat the fervour
And the passion of the Tango.

MRS VERSATILE

They call me 'Mrs Versatile'
I'm not sure if that's true,
But let me tell you a few things
And leave it up to you.

I'm in a ladies' Choir
But don't ask me what I sing,
Soprano, Alto, take your pick
And I'll try anything!

I play the odd recorder piece
I can even play the piano,
I used to play the clarinet
But that was long ago now.

I started dancing years ago
The old Ballroom and Latin,
I've even done a bit of Tap
Some Salsa and Line Dancin'.

I write the odd verse now and then
As I'm clearly demonstrating,
But I don't know if they're good or bad
For loving or for hating!

In truth, I'm 'Good' at many things
But, although I try my best,
You'll find I'm 'Great' at nothing
If you put me to the test!

But it really doesn't matter
Just how well I cannot do,
For all gifts are a blessing
And I'm sharing mine with you.

THE HAIR SALON

The place to go where you can chat
And catch up on the gossip
A place where you can just relax
And let your problems hop it.

The place that always welcomes you
And listens to your story
A place that makes you beautiful
And gives you all the glory.

Your hairdresser is your best friend
When you are in her charge
She'll snip away as time flies by
- Be you small or large.

It's where you go to have a laugh
And get things off your chest
If you want advice, you'll get it
'Cause your hairdresser knows best!

You don't need extra therapy
When you get a salon style
For you don't just get a hairdo
You get service with a smile!

42

FAMILY & FRIENDS
(Attending Choir Concert)

We bid a hearty welcome
To those who freely came,
For those who'd rather be elsewhere
Oh dear, that's such a shame!
We want you to enjoy our show
And join in the odd song,
Perhaps when we have finished
You'll be glad you came along!

We dedicate this to our friends
And family alike,
We hope that you will be impressed
And not 'get on your bike',
We want you all to see
That our work is not in vain,
We'd like you all to listen
With a sense of joy—not pain!

We thank you all for coming
Whether willingly or not,
And although we may be nervous
We'll try not to 'lose the plot',
We may be under pressure
Having been put to the test,
But—whatever happens
You will know we've done our best.

Happy Birthday Andante

This choir was formed some years ago
in 1998,
Our numbers grew and fell again
But we believed in fate.

For even when we were reduced
To only three or four,
Our motto was to 'carry on'
And prove we could do more.

We changed our name and advertised
To get some more recruits,
We're now known as Andante
For we believe this suits.

We've grown again and blossomed
We hope you will agree,
And we're gathered here to celebrate
Our anniversary.

So thank you all for coming
Please join me when I say
"Happy Birthday, Andante"
On this our Special Day!

DECEMBER

This month is full of Christmas Cheer
Of Greetings and Best Wishes;
**This is the month when we can all
Greet everyone with kisses.**

December is the month that means
Eat, drink and be merry;
**December is the only time
The shops sell out of sherry.**

This is the time when we all share
Glad tidings and Good Will;
**This is the time we spend carefree
- Until we see the bill!**

December is for parties
For laughter, joy and fun;
**December is the time of year
When work never gets done.**

But that's not all that Christmas means
There's much more to December,
It celebrates the birth of Christ
And this we should remember.

The time God sent his Son to earth
To teach us right from wrong,
To prove how much He loves us
And hear our praise in song.

CHRISTMAS

Christmas brings us memories
Of loved ones near and far,
It prompts us all to make amends
And heal the deepest scar,
It helps to bring us closer
To those we rarely see,
It fills our hearts with hope and love
To keep eternally.

Christmas brings us comfort
When we think of those we've lost,
It brings healing of the soul
For which Jesus paid the cost,
It offers us forgiveness
For the deeds that we regret,
And reminds us of the good things
That we never should forget.

Christmas is a time of cheer
A time for joy and laughter,
A celebration of Christ's birth
From now to ever after,
So let us all remember
What this time of year is for,
Come on, put on your party hats
And let us sing some more!

CHRISTMASTIME

I was asked to write a poem
To suit this time of year,
A poem that was humorous
And full of Christmas Cheer.

Well, my words may not be funny
But it really seems to me
That all you need are Christmas Lights
And a Whopping Christmas Tree!

A great big Christmas Turkey
With cracker, joke and hat,
Loads of cake and alcohol;
What could be wrong with that?

A time to get together
With long lost friends and foes,
And relatives from near and far
To keep you on your toes.

But it's all too easy to forget,
When gifts are bought and given,
That we celebrate the greatest gift;
The gift of Christ from Heaven.

BIRTHDAY GREETINGS

Your Birthday has again arrived
We need not count the years
The joys of life are wished for you
The smiles, but not the tears
I know it seems like yesterday
When you were in your teens
So make the most of your life now
You know how much it means.

THIRTY-SOMETHING

The time to think
And take account
Of what you've done so far,
The time to sort out
What you want
From life, and who you are.

The time to seek
The truth about
The way your life is going,
The time to wonder
What you'll reap
From seeds you have been sowing.

The time to feel
That someone cares
And values your existence,
The time to give,
As well as take,
Without so much resistance.

The time to realise
How glad
You are to be alive,
The time to look ahead,
Not back;
This is the way to thrive.

LIFE BEGINS AT 40

Life begins at 40
I hope the saying's true!
It surely must depend upon
The things you plan to do.

I thought I couldn't wait until
The kids were grown and gone,
To do the things I couldn't do
When they were very young.

I guess it's still too early
For me to really know
You see, although my kids are grown
They're still living at home!

But when they go, will I be free
To do just as I please?
Or will I find I'm still tied down
To other homely needs.

A partner who is not inclined
To share my zest for life,
Who would much rather spend his time
With his garden, than his wife.

Although this wouldn't sound too bad
If I were old and grey,
I don't think I am ready yet
To 'while' my life away.

I hope this will not be the case
For, if he will not bend,
Far from a new beginning,
For me, 'twill be the end.

50TH BIRTHDAY

For 50 years you have survived
Through good times and through bad,
You've been through all the cycles
Of Son, Husband and Dad.

You're older now and greyer,
You've gained a little weight,
But we all love you, anyway,
Because we think you're great.

The next phase now is 'Granddad',
But this will be, God willing,
Not for quite some time yet
- Or else, there'll be a killing!

And now, it's time to celebrate,
- Calm down, no need to worry,
All we're going to do with you, is . . .
Eat, drink and be merry.

But first, let's toast the Birthday Boy,
'Long Life, Good Health', old sport,
May your life improve with age
Just like a vintage port.

THREE SCORE YEARS
AND TEN

We're gathered here to celebrate
Your three score years and ten,
It's nice to get together
For a booze-up now and then.

There are nuts and crisps and sandwiches
With nibbles, fruit and cake,
Chicken, ham and sausage rolls
Like granny used to make.

You've reached a major milestone
Which we hope you'll well surpass,
May your achievements in the future
Be as great as in the past.

So let us raise our glasses
And drink a toast to you,
We wish you health and happiness
And success in all you do.

YOUNG AT HEART

Why does the body always age
Much faster than the brain?
Why do our joints begin to ache
When it's about to rain?

Why does our spirit still behave
Just like a carefree child?
Why do we think that we can still
Be outrageous and wild?

Who do we think we're kidding
When we try to live our dream?
Our energy has long been spent
And we've run out of steam.

The mind is always willing
But the body's far too weak,
And sometimes we just plain forget
That we have passed our peak.

The younger generation
Will say we are 'young at heart',
But it doesn't really help us
When we start to fall apart.

We'll soon need hip replacements
And lose our teeth and hair,
And then, sooner or later
We'll need constant daily care!

I guess it doesn't matter
What we can or cannot do,
As long as we can still have fun
Our life is not yet through.

FAITH

When you are at your lowest ebb
Please do not despair
Just put your trust in Jesus Christ
And He will hear your prayer.

Things happen for a reason
And sometimes it's a test
By staying true and faithful
You'll be forever blessed.

We pray that God will make you well
And that your faith will grow
But what He has in store for you
Is not for us to know.

Remember all your blessings
Each one a precious gift
Think of all your loved ones
And your spirit will soon lift.

Have courage, strength and patience
And trust the Lord above
For only He can make things right
His Mercy and His Love.

NEVER TOO LATE

If you had studied more at school
You'd now be home and dry,
Not hopping from place to place
Like an 'odd job' kind of guy.

You could have gone so very far
You could have been so smart,
You didn't try too hard at school
- You were only keen on Art!

You've tried so many different things
From stylist to mechanic,
But you never lasted anywhere
- If I were you I'd panic!

You're certainly not stupid
And you're learning thick and fast,
That it really is never too late
To make up for the past.

I know you dream of better times
We want that for you too,
I pray one day you will succeed
- But it's really up to you!

I THINK OF YOU LONELY

I think of you lonely
By night and by day,
I think of you wiping
Your tear-drops away,
I think of you wishing
That you hadn't been
A member and party
To that horrible scene.

I think of you cursing
The hour that you woke
And answered the call;
You thought it a joke,
I think of you kicking
Yourself in your sleep,
Who'd ever have thought
You'd be in it so deep!

I think of you asking
What tempted you so,
The answer is one
That only you know,
I think of you sad
When our letters you get,
I think this experience
You'll never forget.

I think of you lonely
By night and by day,
I write, but in letters
I fear I can't say
How much we all miss you,
How much we all care,
I hope that, in future,
In mind this you'll bear.

TURN TO GOD, AND PRAY

I don't know what to say to you
I don't know what to do,
I wish I had a magic wand
To make your dreams come true.

I don't know how to help you
I don't know if I dare,
No matter what we try to do
You still think we don't care.

You know, it's really up to you
To turn your life around,
If you don't want to listen
Then you won't hear a sound.

We're going round in circles
And getting nowhere fast,
We should be looking forward
Not dwelling on the past.

So please let's try and celebrate
The birth of each new day,
If you don't want to talk to us
Then turn to God, and pray.

CRY OF DESPAIR

What did we ever do to you
That you should be this way?
Why do you turn away from us
No matter what we say?

What happened to your loyalty
Your honour and your zeal?
I really thought you would succeed
But nothing now seems real.

We have bent over backwards
To try and help you out,
But you won't even talk to us
You only want to shout.

You know we love you dearly
Why do you treat us so?
Please tell us all your troubles
We really want to know.

We may not have the answer
But at least we'll understand,
And if you make the effort
Then we'll give a helping hand.

God helps those who help themselves
But you must make the start,
If you need strength and courage
You must seek it from the heart.

THE TRUTH—AT LAST!

You feel you've been hard done by
That fate has struck a blow,
But what you've made us suffer
You will never know.

You feared you'd be rejected
But our love never failed,
You didn't put your trust in us
And that's why you 'de-railed'.

You sought to find your comfort
From strangers here and there,
But they could only lead you
To hardship and despair.

Self pity and resentment
Are cancers of the soul,
When you forgive and start to live
Then you will become 'whole'.

Don't hide away your troubles
Don't bury them deep down,
Let them out, once and for all,
And turn your life around.

The ball is in your court now
It's really up to you,
All we can do is hope and pray
That you will see this through.

But what you should remember
Is, despite what's in the past,
You always will be one of us
And that's the truth—at last!

I hope I haven't bored you
I've tried to be sincere,
Your life is precious, live it well,
God bless and keep you near.

A Plea From The Heart

We love you dearly, but . . .
You never listen to what we say
You have temper tantrums every day,
You always seem to be on the defence
And you never use your common sense.

We love you dearly, but . . .
You never treat us with respect
You always do things you'll regret,
You hurt our feelings, come what may,
And you leave the house in disarray.

We love you dearly, but . . .
The only time you're nice to us
Is when you're after some more cash,
You don't appreciate what you've got
All you do is blow the lot.

We love you dearly, but . . .
You expect too much from us, my dear,
You take advantage all through the year,
You're not prepared to do your share
You're selfish and you do not care.

We love you dearly, but . . .
It would be a great relief
If you'd turn over a new leaf,
We'd forget what's gone before
And we would love you all the more.

DON'T TAKE ME FOR GRANTED

Don't take me for granted
Just because you can,
You know how much I love you
'Cause I'm your biggest fan.

Don't take me for granted
Just because I'm near,
You know that I'll do anything
As long as I am here.

Don't take me for granted
Don't take me for a song,
Just because it's easy
You still know it is wrong.

Don't take me for granted
Just because I'm game,
You know I'd never let you down
But can you say the same?

Don't take me for granted
Just spare a thought or two,
The time will come when I'll no longer
Be around for you.

Don't take me for granted
What planet are you on?
Our time on earth is precious, and
You'll miss me when I'm gone!

THE YEARS HAVE BEEN AND GONE

The day you left was full of lies
Why did you take the blame?
We thought you had destroyed our lives
We looked at you with shame.

You did not justify your claims
When they were so denied,
So what were we supposed to think?
Except that you had lied.

I did not know that you were there
On my wedding day,
I felt so saddened when I heard
That you'd been turned away.

I miss the talks we used to have
I miss the games we played,
I miss the way you looked at me
When I misbehaved.

I'm sorry for the years we've lost
We could have been so close,
But you were never there for me;
This I regret the most.

I wish you could have been there
When the boys were growing up,
They've never known the luxury
Of sitting on granddad's lap.

It is too late to make amends
The years have been and gone,
But still, I hope we can be friends
From this moment on.

WHY BOTHER?

The more you're relied on
The more you are scorned
The more you are needed
The deeper the wound
The more you are given
The more you return
You may as well give up
And be on your own.

The more you seek friendship
Trust and respect
The more you find sadness
Deceit and neglect
You try to be helpful
But all is in vain
- You'll only be taken
For granted again!

HOPE

What do we have in this life
That makes us feel so gay?
Why do we continue to
Look forward to each day?
What is it that makes us think
That we have much to say?
Why is it that we're so sure
Our problems will not stay?

Love is what makes us so gay
But with it, too, comes grief;
Dreams help us to face each day
But each day is too brief;
Confidence gives us our say
But we're not always right;
Faith makes problems go away
But they're never out of sight.

Hope is one thing that can help
It gives us all a chance
To look ahead at what might be
And not at what was once,
A chance to see that, if you try
To make a better life,
You need not throw your dreams away,
You need not use the knife!

THE GIFT OF LIFE

To celebrate the gift of life
And make the most of living,
To reap the benefits and joys
And the rewards of giving,
We are surely duty bound
To go as far as poss.,
To stretch our limits to the full
And avoid that sense of loss.

To trust our natural instincts,
To open every door,
To bravely go where no-one else
Has dared to go before,
To recognise potential
And have courage to pursue,
But most of all, to have faith
In everything we do.

It could take a lifetime
To realise the truth,
That dreams and fantasies are not
Exclusive to the youth,
For young and old alike can feel
The joy or pain and sorrow
Of looking back with their regrets,
Or forward to tomorrow.

The gift of life is something
Which really should be treasured,
There is nothing, here on earth,
By which it can be measured,
So let us live it to the full
And pray for peace worldwide,
That we may live in harmony
Together, side by side.

HEAVEN!

To stroke the petal of a rose
To smell the morning dew
To sink into a symphony
And dream of days with you.

To lie beneath a clear blue sky
To hear the birds in song
To feel the sunshine in your hair
And want to sing along.

To splash about in waters deep
To hear the sea-gulls cry
To drift upon the sea of time
With thoughts of you and I.

This must be what heaven's like
So peaceful, still and calm
So full of love and goodness
-Whoops! There goes my alarm!

TIME

What leads us to the path we take?
What is our guiding force?
Is it what we call 'Destiny'
Or just Time that takes its course?

I look back on the years gone by
And wonder where they went,
I'm older, but no wiser,
And my energy is spent.

I cannot help but feel remorse
For the things I haven't done,
I always thought there would be time
But Time is on the run.

I tell myself that it is Fate
What must be, must be,
I try my best to be content
But still I am not free.

Deep down I know there must be more
And so I tell my chums:
"There's a brighter day tomorrow"
But Tomorrow never comes.

WHAT DO I WANT?

There are so many things
I still want to do
If only I had the time,
There are so many things
I still want to see
And so many mountains to climb.

I've already wasted
So many years
Putting things off till tomorrow,
If I'd make an effort
To follow my dreams
Perhaps I would not feel so hollow.

I'd like to be happy
Jolly and gay
Without a care in the world,
I'd like to be free
Of unpleasant thoughts,
Be warm and never cold.

I want to sing
I want to dance
I want to learn to skate,
I want to travel
Around the world
Before it is too late.

I want to have fun
To wine and dine
And try every dish in the land,
I want to have everything
Money can buy
And live a life so grand.

I'd like to meet
'Prince Charming'
And experience true romance,
I'd like to be
Adventurous
And try everything—once!

BUT WAIT!

If all my wishes
Did come true
What difference would it make
If, when I die,
I did not have
A soul that God could take?

The most important
Wish of all
Is to have Jesus in my heart,
That He may guide me
Day by day
Never to depart.

BLESS US, LORD

Oh Lord, I thank Thee with my heart
For all that I possess,
I hope to make good use of them
And ask Thee these to bless . . . .

My **Husband**, that he may be good
And kind as all should be,
That I may always mean as much
To him, as he to me.

Our **Sons**, that we may watch them grow
And look at them with pride,
May they have health and happiness
And a good wife by their side.

Our **Home**, that we may always have
A roof over our heads,
Keep it safe from fire and theft
Make it secure instead.

Bless **Me**, Lord, that I may be
A worthy wife and mother,
Help me to be dutiful
And not too tired to bother.

But most of all Lord, bless our **Love**
That it may always be,
The greatest thing that we possess
The dearest thing to me.

PERHAPS

Perhaps one day the sun will shine
Without making us sweat
Perhaps one day the rain will fall
Without getting us wet
Perhaps one day we'll eat our fill
And not put on the weight
Perhaps one day we'll learn to love
The one we love to hate.

Be careful what you wish for
I've often heard it said
For what you think you want the most
Can bring heartache instead
Be grateful for the things you have
The things we take for granted
For we are better off than most
Our blessings should be counted.

Perhaps now is the time to see
The light that shines within
Perhaps it's time to realise
Not everything's a sin
Perhaps the time has come at last
To embrace the life we're given
And make the most of each new day
Always, 24/7.

THE LOTTERY

What makes you think that all I want
Is money, money, money?
The Lottery is just a game
Don't get too heavy, honey!

Who wants to win the Lottery
And be so stinking rich,
That everyone resents you
And thinks you are a bitch?

A little wouldn't go amiss
I must admit, that's true,
There's plenty one can spend it on,
I would, and so would you.

But too much is a curse, for sure
For with it too comes trouble,
And with no friends to turn to
Your worries would be double.

We all think we have suffered
Our share of trouble and strife,
But the greatest Lottery of all
Is the one that we call 'Life'.

So let us count our blessings
Let our disillusion end,
For we're richer in the things we have;
The things we cannot spend.

Like love, respect and friendship
Trust and freedom too,
Achieving goals and taking pride
In everything we do.

Rewards for these are worth much more
Than anything money can buy,
The greatest gifts one can possess
Are free to you and I.

THE GANG

Hey, you, with that bottle of beer,
Come here,
Tell me why you drink so much;
So you can't keep in touch
With reality?
That's a pity!

Hey, you, with that big black eye,
Why . . .
Did you get in that fight?
You know it's not right,
But still,
You will!

Hey, you, with that ring in your nose,
You know how it goes,
Life is a vicious circle, and so
Why do you go
On that merry-go-round?
—In for a penny, in for a pound?

Hey, you lot, cut out than din,
You know you can't win,
Round up the others
And go to your mothers;
How much more do you think we can take?
Sort out your lives, for goodness sake!

THERE, BUT FOR
THE GRACE . . .

Make way for a budding failure
Make way for a 'down and out',
Step out of the way, but do not ask
What his life is all about.

Don't look at him as you pass him by
Don't let your heart see the pain,
There's a sad and lonely look in his eye
And you'll only feel guilty again.

Treat him as if he doesn't exist
Treat him as if he's not there,
Do not acknowledge the state he's in
Or he may think that you care.

Tell yourself it's his own fault
Tell yourself he's to blame,
He must have done something to deserve
Living a life of shame.

You think it could never happen to you
You think you'll always be fine,
But remember . . .
There, but for the grace of God,
Go you—or I—or mine.

Have A Heart!

We prey on our misfortunes
We're always full of woe,
The slightest thing that may go wrong
Will leave us feeling low.

We feel let down so easily
We expect so much from others,
But what do we give in return
To our fellow brothers?

When suffering confronts us
We look the other way,
We never stop to offer help
We just think "go away".

If only we could see the pain
Perhaps, then, we could find
A little kindness in our hearts
And not be quite so blind.

We'd see that we're so fortunate
Compared with many souls,
We'd thank the Lord for what we had
And change our very goals.

We'd take advantage of our gifts,
We'd even beg or borrow,
To do, today, the most we could
And not wait till tomorrow.

GOOD LUCK?

Good Luck is always followed
By Bad Luck in the end,
So is it worth the agony
Of trying to pretend?

There's no such thing as 'Good Luck'
It's Bad Luck in disguise,
Where Good Luck lies you'll always find
There's sadness in the eyes.

You may try to win fortunes
But then, when this you do,
You end up losing other things
Far more precious to you.

Would you rather riches
Than happiness and health?
Or do you value family
Less than you do your wealth?

If Good Luck came to you one day
Of course, you would rejoice,
But if Bad Luck took your love away
Then what would be your choice?

Wealth and fortunes are but dust
Compared to those you love,
So treasure them and be content
And trust the Lord above.

WHY IS IT ALWAYS ME?

When there are problems to resolve
Like what is meant to be
When people need a helping hand
Or a cat's stuck up a tree
When someone needs a favour
Or just wants a cup of tea
When they need someone to turn to . . .
Why is it always me?

When couples are in trouble
And need help to sort things out
When things aren't going well at home
And all they do is shout
When they cannot stop complaining
And just want to be set free
When they need someone to talk to . . .
Why is it always me?

When people feel hard done by
And that life just isn't fair
When they seek to fill the gaps in life
But simply do not care
Who they hurt along the way
- Perhaps they cannot see!
When someone's getting trodden on . . .
Why is it always me?

When there's bad luck to be dished out
When something must go wrong
When there is no umbrella
And the rain becomes a storm
When love goes by unnoticed
Because one's too blind to see
When someone must be last in line . . .
Why is it always me!

LORD, GIVE ME STRENGTH

Dear Lord,

You've always been there
When I've needed you
I've never yet given up hope,
You've always given me
Courage, dear Lord,
And, somehow, the strength to cope.

You've answered my prayers
Many times before
You've helped me through many a trial,
And, Lord, I know
That it's thanks to you
I've got through with a smile.

So now in my moment
Of need, again,
I beg you to show me the way,
Give me the strength
And the courage, Lord,
To cope with each new day.

Amen.

SILVER LINING

There's a silver lining
On the edge of every cloud
Like a guardian angel in the rain,
It turns every disaster
Into something more profound
And lets us see the healing through the pain.

We always feel hard done by
When tragedy occurs
And figure that our luck has just run out,
But if we took the time
To consider all the odds
We'd know a higher force was thereabout.

We should never grumble
When things seem to go wrong
Or whether we need doctor or a nurse,
For, whatever happens,
And however bad we feel
There's always someone, somewhere, feeling worse.

There's a silver lining
On the edge of every cloud
That's waiting for a crisis to appear,
It will then enfold us
To cushion every blow
And breathe a sigh of hope for every tear.

IF ONLY . . .

If only I were tall and slim
With skin so smooth and fair,
Elegant and graceful
With long and shiny hair.

If only I were more in tune
With current modes and trends,
I wouldn't feel so 'out of it'
When talking to my friends.

If only I knew when to stand
And speak my mind outright,
When to keep my mouth shut
And stay out of the fight.

If only I could understand
The basic rules of life,
The secrets of good motherhood;
How to be a perfect wife.

If only I could be content
With what my life has been
And recognise some value
In the things I've done and seen.

If only I could start again
And live my life anew,
I'd not repeat the same mistakes
I'd know just what to do.

If only I knew how to love
With total heart and soul
And be loved, likewise, in return;
Then, surely, I'd be whole.

DO OR DIE

When nothing seems to go your way
And no-one seems to care,
When people do not listen
And don't even know you're there,
When your feelings do not matter
To anyone around,
And your muffled sobbing's
Just an irritating sound.

When your heart is almost breaking
And your tears won't keep their place,
When you try to stop your shaking
And depart the scene with grace,
When inside you can't stop screaming
But the sound will not release,
When you want to run a mile
But your feet are treading grease.

When you stop to look around you
But you cannot see a soul,
When you hold your hand out for support
But sink deeper in the hole,
When the crowds disperse and pass you by
Without a second glance,
When you feel like giving up on life
That you do not stand a chance.

When you think you can't take any more
And are pulling out your hair,
When you long for warmth and comfort
But are drowning in despair . . . .

- STOP -

That's the time to hold your head up
Look the world right in the eye,
Show them what you're really made of
- From now on it's "Do or Die".

My Sword And Shield

With every step I take, I feel
No nearer to my goal,
My hopes and fears are ever real
And rest deep in my soul.

I know not what to say or do
To make things come my way,
I only pray to God on high
That I will have my day.

I try to make the most of life
And not waste any chances,
But who's to say that what we snub
Are not worth second glances?

I cannot ever give up hope,
It is my sword and shield,
I must believe that, one fine day,
My fate will be revealed.

FAME AND FORTUNE

I don't want fame and fortune
I don't want hoards of gold,
Just want a chance to find myself
Before I grow too old.

I don't want lots of money
Don't want designer gear,
Just want to look and feel good
As long as I am here.

Don't want to be an Idol
Don't want to be a Star,
Just want to be remembered
By people near and far.

I only ask for wisdom
I do not ask for wealth,
I want what money cannot buy
Like happiness and health.

I want my cup to overflow
With kindness and goodwill,
That I may spread it all around
And all can have their fill.

OH, WHAT A SIN!

What do you think of
When sitting alone
With nothing to do
But stay at home?
What do you think of
When no-one is in
But you and the telly?
Oh, what a sin!

Patience is tried
But sometimes it fails
Sitting alone
Starts you biting your nails,
No-one to talk to
By day or by night
So you just go to bed
'Cause you don't want a fight.

The door slowly opens
He's come home at last
Drunk as a lord
Just like in the past,
You swallow your sobs
So he thinks you're asleep
He falls to the floor
And you can't help but weep.

Was this the man
You knew when you married?
You should have thought harder,
You shouldn't have hurried,
But love him you do
And fade it will never
For this is the man
You will care for forever.

THANKS!?!

Thank you for the things you say
That make me feel no good,
Thank you for reminding me
To do the chores I should,
Thank you for helping me see
That all is not quite right,
And thank you for not caring
Just how late I work at night.

Thank you for the things I lack
To help with daily chores,
Thanks for leaving me to cope
With those three kids of ours,
Thanks for not taking away
The 'joys' of motherhood,
And thank you for not sharing work
That any husband would.

Thank you for complaining
When the ironing isn't done,
Thank you for ignoring me
When I would like some fun,
Thank you for falling asleep
In front of the TV,
And thanks for shouting insults
When I wake you for your tea!

Thank you for not spoiling me
With gifts that say "You're great",
Thank you for not wanting me
To stay out after eight,
Thank you for not giving me
Some time to call my own,
And thanks for demonstrating that
My place is in the home!

Gee – Thanks!

TILL DEATH US DO PART

I'd like to come home
To a house full of cheer,
I'd like to relax
With a lager or beer,
I'd like to be greeted
With words soft and sweet
And I'd like not to argue
Each time that we meet.

I'd like you to realise
That pain cannot speak,
I'd like you to know
That it's help that I seek,
I'd like you to see
You're not always correct
And I'd like you to show me
A little respect.

I'd like you to listen
When I've something to say,
I'd like you to praise me
At least once a day,
I'd like you to notice
If I am not there
And I'd like you to worry
And show that you care.

I'd like you to think of
The day we were wed,
I'd like you to remember
The words we both said,
I'd like you to tell me
That you spoke from the heart
And I'd like you to love me
"Till Death Us Do Part".

Driving Me To Drink!

If there were any way at all
To make you realise
The hurt you cause me every day
I'm sure you'd be surprised.

For when you say "I love you"
And "You're the only girl for me"
I can't help but believe it
For I love you too, you see.

But when you hold me tight at night
And whisper words so sweet
I know that you will fail, again,
Your promises to keep.

I wish you would remember
All the kind things that you say
And act as if you meant them
For it doesn't seem that way.

So please, next time you feel the urge
To moan—just stop and think
Before you criticise again,
'Cause you're driving me to drink!

PUSHING ME AWAY

You tell me that you love me
But you never treat me so,
All you do is criticise
And tell me where to go.

I sometimes wonder where I'd be
If not married to you,
Have I wasted all these years
Not knowing what to do?

I've tried to make the best of things
I've tried to be content,
But you never made it easy
And I wish you would repent.

But you are far too stubborn
And you always think you're right,
You will not listen to my views
And all we do is fight.

I know I also have my faults
And we must share the blame,
But surely, after all these years
We'd have learnt to play the game.

You tell me that you love me
It's an easy thing to say,
But actions speak louder than words
And they're pushing me away.

SECOND CHANCE

Once there was love, compassion and care,
Respect and opinions mattered,
But now our feelings are never shared
Our thoughts and dreams are scattered.

When did we go so far astray?
When did our paths separate?
Why didn't anyone warn us
That love can turn to hate.

We are like ships that pass in the night
One's home when the other's at work,
But when we're together, we always fight
And act like a fool and a jerk!

We've entered a vicious circle
And cannot seem to get out,
Whenever one of us tries to get near
The other just wants to shout.

This isn't a 'one-way' street we are on,
We can reverse and go back,
If we are both willing to make a 'U-turn'
Perhaps we can get back on track.

Forget all the bad times and build on the good,
Bring back some good old romance,
If we treat each other like partners should,
We might have a second chance.

ALONE IN MY ROOM

One day as I sat all alone in my room
I gazed at a picture of me and my groom,
We looked oh so young, so carefree and gay
On that wet Sunday morning in the middle of May.

I took it and held it so close to my breast
And once more I cried, it's the thing I do best,
For the memory of the day we were wed
Brought such pain to my heart that more tears I did shed.

The joy, the happiness and the romance
Is not the same as it was once,
For all that is left of the love that we shared
Are the kids—to remind us that once we cared.

And so, as I sat all alone in my room
Hugging the picture of me and my groom,
The door slowly opened and I heard a voice say
"Well, this is it, I'm going away".

If only I'd had the courage to say
"Darling, I love you, I want you to stay",
Then maybe he, too, would have wanted to try
To work things out, and not say "Good-bye".

Yesteryear

I lie awake at night and think
Of what was yesteryear,
The joy, the fun, the love we had
It seemed to be so dear.

We laughed a lot and cried a lot
Our thoughts we always shared,
I never ever doubted you
I really thought you cared.

But all that is behind us now
Our paths have grown apart,
All that remains are memories
And a slight pain in my heart.

I lie awake at night and think
Of what was yesteryear,
And try to work out what went wrong
As I wipe away a tear.

VALENTINE

Oh, Valentine, where are you?
When will you come to me?
I see you in my future
You are my destiny.

Oh, Valentine, I cannot wait,
Until the day we meet,
For you to take me by surprise
And sweep me off my feet.

Come soon to me, dear Valentine
And make my dreams come true,
For I have waited all my life
For such a man as you.

LOVE IS JUST AROUND THE CORNER

I've always tried to do what's right
I've always tried to cope
My sense of duty is so deep
But, still, I dare to hope.

I am ever the optimist
Who believes in love and fate
And that, 'round every corner'
Is somebody's special mate.

One day I'll turn a corner
And find I'm next in line
For that special someone waiting there
Will turn out to be mine!

TRUE LOVE

What is the meaning of 'true love'?
How can it be defined?
How can we be sure it's real
And not just in our mind?

How do we uncover it
From wherever it may hide?
And then, how can we keep it
Forever by our side?

How do we describe it?
Love is fragile; Love is strong;
It brings sadness; it brings joy;
It is where we all belong.

Love cannot be ordered
Delivered, sold or bought,
But it can be discarded
Without a second thought.

What goes around, comes around
So, if the saying's true,
When you give your love freely,
It will find its way to you.

OUR LAST WALK

The stars that night were none too bright
The rain was almost sleet,
I looked up and your eyes met mine
And my heart missed a beat.

We walked along that windy lane
But all that I could feel,
Was your left arm around my waist
And time, for me, stood still.

We stopped outside my home address
You kissed me in the rain,
Reluctantly, we said 'Goodnight'
And you kissed me once again.

I waved to you as you walked off
Your eyes did not leave mine,
You reached halfway across the street
But then, there was no time . . .

No time for you to see the car
That came in such a rage,
No time for me to scream or warn
And yet—it seemed an age.

I ran to you and held you tight
I panicked and I cried,
You smiled at me and drew me close
And, with one last kiss, you died.

The stars tonight are none too bright
The rain is almost sleet,
As I remember our last walk
Along this lonely street.

DIANA

The world will seem an empty place
When we no longer see her face,
Now that she is but a dream
This is how the world will seem:

Like a candle with no wick
Like a clock that doesn't tick,
Like a forest without trees
Like a beehive without bees.
Like a tunnel with no light
Like a boxer with no fight,
Like a TV with no screen
Like a palace with no queen.

She stood out among the rest
And never failed to try her best
To comfort those who were in pain;
She could not live her life in vain.

She fought through all the madness
Despite her pain and sadness,
And, with the love she freely shared,
She showed the world she really cared.

Her smile will live forevermore
But we will miss her, that's for sure,
Despite her role of many parts
She really was a Queen of Hearts.

As far back as we can see
Her happiness was not to be,
Now that she's found her release
I pray that she may rest in peace.

TRIBUTE TO BABY 'P'

What is this cruelty within?
What motive does it serve?
How can such torture be dished out?
Who could have such a nerve?

A helpless child with broken bones
Who knows not what the cause is,
Who never felt a mother's love
Only the cuts and bruises.

We are in shock, we want to cry
"What sheer madness is this?"
When a baby cries, it surely wants
A cuddle and a kiss!

But instead of words of comfort
And being soothingly caressed,
The child's continued suffering
Is put further to the test.

Perhaps it is a blessing
That this child's life was so short,
We hope that those who were to blame
Are served justice by the Court.

I pray to God that this child's soul
Will find its way to Heaven,
Where it will have the peace and love
That on earth was never given.

UNTIL WE MEET AGAIN

There are no words that can describe
The way that we all feel,
Our world has suddenly collapsed
And nothing now seems real.

Your parting brought us nothing
But confusion, pain and sorrow,
Our thoughts dwell only on the past
We cannot face tomorrow.

You've left a gap in all our lives
A space we cannot fill,
You touched the hearts of everyone
With your kindness and goodwill.

But this should be a tribute
For the gifts you've left behind,
Your family and grandchildren
And your love of all mankind.

You've set a great example
For all of us to follow,
And this will give us courage
To cope with each tomorrow.

There's nothing left to say, dear friend,
Except, come shine or rain,
We pray that you will Rest in Peace
Until we meet again.

In Memory Of A Grandmother

(On behalf of the grandchildren)

We haven't come to say 'Goodbye'
We've come to say 'Farewell'
You've started a new life in Heaven
And left behind your shell.

You've suffered hard times in the past
But no-one kept a score
The memories you've left behind
Will live forevermore.

Your hospitality at home
Was more than just a token
When people came from near and far
Your door was always open.

Your family always came first
You looked at them with pride
Especially your grandchildren
We were always by your side.

You were always there for us
You taught us right from wrong
Your kindness and your love for us
Will keep us going strong.

We may no longer see your face
And this will cause us pain
But we know you're in a better place
And your life was not in vain.

Your influence will stay with us
And forever be our guide
So Rest in Peace, God Bless and Keep you
Ever by His side.

CLOSURE

When you were young and handsome
With a fine wife by your side,
You couldn't help but stray
With loose women far and wide.

When you became a family
With a daughter and two sons,
It didn't stop you gambling
And losing all your funds.

You broke up from your family
And went to pastures new,
You turned your back on all of us
But still, we prayed for you.

We wanted to look up to you
We wanted to be proud,
But you were never there for us
We lived under a cloud.

And yet, in recent months
When we thought we had you back,
You had to let us down again
And give us all 'the sack'.

You weren't the greatest husband
And you weren't the greatest dad,
But, deep down, we still loved you
So you can't have been that bad.

We know that God forgives our sins
And we forgive you too,
We pray that you are in God's hands
And Peace is now with you.

WHAT IS OUR LIFE?

The days go by so quietly
The nights go by unseen,
But do we stop to wonder
What all our life has been?

Does it have a meaning?
Does it have a goal?
Or do we let it pass us by
Without a thought at all?

Why waste our years on this here earth?
Why let our aims escape us?
For who knows what there lies ahead
Beyond that final exodus.

ONE THING WE KNOW . . .

The sun may shine
Upon the earth
The wind may do its deed,
But these are all
Predictable
It's we who should take heed.

The moon may rise
To give us light
The rain may flood the ground,
But when we're told
To be prepared
We do not hear a sound.

We live each day
In ignorance
Of what may lie ahead,
We care not for
One thing we know . . .
One day we shall be dead.

TO BE OR NOT TO BE?

Why were we put upon this earth?
Why go to all that trouble?
If all we can look forward to
Is ending up as rubble.

Why teach our children right from wrong?
Why show them joy and laughter?
If all we have is 'here and now'
And there is no 'ever after'.

How can we make some sense of this?
How can we understand?
When day by day we're living with
Heads buried in the sand.

There is a greater force at work
A power we cannot fight,
And if we open up our hearts
The truth will come to light.

God sent his son to teach us
How to love our fellow brother,
He came to grant forgiveness
For our sins to one another.

There is an 'ever after'
And it's waiting for the day
When our time is up and we accept
That we are on our way.

Our way to everlasting life
When we, at last, will see,
That, through Christ, our place in Paradise
Was always meant to be.

102

LIFE?

See
Hear
Smell
Fear

Lows
Highs
Memories
Lies

Smiles
Deeds
Thoughts
Needs

Hope
Joy
Pain
Death

- Peace -

These poems were written
from the heart
(but not, necessarily,
from personal experience)

I hope you have enjoyed them!

Theo S.